A COMPASSIONATE CALL TO

COUNTER CULTURE

IN A WORLD OF

POVERTY • SAME-SEX MARRIAGE • RACISM

SEX SLAVERY • IMMIGRATION • PERSECUTION

ABORTION • ORPHANS • PORNOGRAPHY

DAVID PLATT

NEW YORK TIMES BESTSELLING AUTHOR

LifeWay Press®
Nashville, Tennessee

Published by LifeWay Press®
© 2015 David Platt
Reprinted June 2016, April 2018, July 2018

Requests for permission should be addressed in writing to
LifeWay Press, One LifeWay Plaza, Nashville, TN 37234.

ISBN: 9781430032557
Item number: P005647993

Dewey Decimal Classification Number: 248.83
Subject Heading: CHRISTIANITY \ CHRISTIANITY AND CULTURE \ SOCIAL ISSUES

Printed in the United States of America

Student Ministry Publishing
LifeWay Resources
One LifeWay Plaza
Nashville, TN 37234

We believe that the Bible has God for its author; salvation for its end;
and truth, without any mixture of error, for its matter
and that all Scripture is totally true and trustworthy.
To review LifeWay's doctrinal guideline,
please visit *www.lifeway.com/doctrinalguideline*.

Photo of David Platt: Allison Lewis

CONTENTS

ABOUT THE AUTHOR

DR. DAVID PLATT, President of the International Mission Board, is deeply devoted to Christ and His Word. David's first love in ministry is making disciples, sharing, showing, and teaching God's Word in everyday life. He has traveled extensively to serve alongside church leaders throughout the United States and around the world.

A life-long learner, David has earned two undergraduate and three advanced degrees. He holds a Bachelor of Arts (B.A.) and Bachelor of Arts in Journalism (A.B.J.) from the University of Georgia, and a Master of Divinity (M.Div.), Master of Theology (Th.M), and Doctor of Philosophy (Ph.D) from New Orleans Baptist Theological Seminary. He previously served at New Orleans Baptist Theological Seminary as Dean of Chapel and Assistant Professor of Expository Preaching and Apologetics, Staff Evangelist at Edgewater Baptist Church in New Orleans, and eight years as the Senior Pastor of The Church at Brook Hills in Birmingham, AL. David has written several books, *Radical, Radical Together, Follow Me,* and most recently *Counter Culture*.

David founded Radical (*Radical.net*), a ministry devoted to serving churches and disseminating disciple-making resources toward the end that the gospel might be made known in all nations.

David and his wife Heather have four children: Caleb, Joshua, Mara Ruth, and Isaiah.

This Bible study is adapted from David Platt's book, *Counter Culture*, and from the teaching videos in this study.

CULTURE
CULTURE

START

On popular issues like poverty and slavery, where Christians are likely to be applauded for our social action, we're quick to stand up and speak out. Yet on controversial issues like homosexuality and abortion, where Christians are likely to be criticized for our social action, we are content to sit down and stay quiet. It's as if we've decided to pick and choose which social issues we'll contest in our culture and which we'll concede. And our picking and choosing normally revolves around what is most comfortable—and least costly—for us in the culture around us.

What if the main issue is not poverty or sex trafficking, homosexuality or abortion? What if the main issue is God? What if the main issue is the glory of God revealed in the gospel? And what might happen if we made Him our focus instead? In a world marked by sex slavery and sexual immorality, the abandonment of children and the murder of children, racism and persecution, the needs of the poor and the neglect of the widow, how would we act if we fixed our gaze on the holiness, love, goodness, truth, justice, authority, and mercy of God revealed in the gospel?

If we did, we would recognize that the same heart of God that moves us to war against sex trafficking also moves us to war against sexual immorality. We would discover that the same gospel that compels us to combat poverty also compels us to defend marriage. We would discover that a number of apparently separate issues are, in fact, all intimately connected to our understanding of who God is and how God relates to everything around us. When our focus turns to God, our hearts shift from what is most comfortable. Instead, our lives are fixed on what is most glorifying to God, and in Him we will find far greater reward than anything our culture could ever offer us. To be students who radically follow Jesus with conviction, courage, and compassion, we must learn to live counter culturally.

For more insight on this week's topic, read the introduction and chapter 1 of David Platt's book *Counter Culture* (Tyndale, 2015).

WATCH

Complete the viewer guide below as you watch DVD Session 1.

TWO PRAYERS FROM ACTS 17

1. God, make us zealous for Your _____.

- _____ of the universe

- _____ of life

- _____ of the nations

- _____ of the needy

- _____ of each of us

- _____ over all of us

- _____ of the world

2. God, make us passionate for people's _____.

FIVE TRUTHS OF THE GOSPEL

1. _____ of God: God is the holy, just, and gracious Creator of all things.

2. _____ of man: we're each created by God, but we're all corrupted by sin.

3. _____ of Christ: Jesus alone is able to remove our sin and reconcile us to God.

4. _____ of faith: the way to be reconciled to God is through faith in Jesus.

5. _____ of eternity: our eternal destiny is dependent on our response to Jesus.

RESPOND

We live in a difficult time. The culture around us is increasingly resistant to Christ and the church. Too often Christians sit by silently as a war rages over social issues from abortion to homosexuality to sex trafficking and poverty. But we can no longer remain silent if we believe the gospel.

So how can we be a generation of students who are compassionate and courageous in this battle? We must begin by being zealous for God's glory.

In the Book of Acts we learn that Paul engaged in this war about cultural issues in the city of Athens. The city was filled with idols/gods and Paul's response in Acts 17:16 is clear.

"Now while Paul was waiting for them at Athens, his spirit was provoked within him as he saw that the city was full of idols." –Acts 17:16

Why do you think Paul experienced holy anger when he saw the idols in Athens?

How would verses like Isaiah 42:8 have impacted Paul's response to the idols in Athens?

When we truly believe that God alone deserves all praise and all glory, then something deep rises up in us, and we cannot stay silent when we see idols all around us. While the idols in Paul's context were literal statues representing false gods, the idols of our day can be much more subtle. Rather than statues of false gods, students today worship idols like self, sports, success, or money.

List at least five "idols" that you see students around you worshiping in place of God:
1.
2.
3.
4.
5.

As a result of seeing the idols throughout Athens, Paul could not stay silent, so he was driven into the synagogue, into the streets, and eventually up to Mars Hill, around the high philosophers of Rome. Before we look at Paul's response to the philosophers, we need to consider our response to the idol worship that goes on around us every day.

Why do we ignore those living in poverty in our community?

Why do we disregard orphans and widows?

Why do we tolerate or excuse abortion in our culture?

Why do we stay silent on homosexuality and so-called same-sex marriage?

The answer to each of these questions is rooted in idolatry. We ignore the poor because we idolize wealth, luxury, and comfort. How do the other issues listed show our idolatry?

ISSUE:
Ignoring those in poverty

IDOL:
Wealth/luxury/comfort

Disregarding orphans and widows

Tolerating abortion

Staying silent on same-sex marriage

When we recognize that idolatry lies at the root of all these issues, we realize that the reason we must fight these issues is because we're zealous for the glory of God. Are our hearts provoked with a longing for God to be glorified in our world? We fight these battles in our culture by connecting our desire for justice and mercy to His glory.

We must work for justice in the world...why? Because we want God to be exalted as the Judge of the world. We must show God's mercy to the world...why? Because we want God to be exalted as the Savior of the world.

Let's look again at Acts and see Paul's response to the philosophers of his day. Paul simply told the people of Athens about God and His glory.

Consider the seven characteristics of God that Paul shared with the philosophers in Athens. We touched on these briefly in the video, but let's make sure we understand the significance of each one. Read the following verses and list the characteristic Paul was highlighting:

Read Acts 17:22-24.

God is the _____ of the universe.

Read verse 25.

God is the _____ of life.

Read verse 26.

God is the _____ of the nations.

Read verse 27.

God is the _____ of the needy.

Read verse 28.

God is the _____ of each of us.

Read verse 29.

God is the _____ over all of us.

Read verses 30-31.

God is the _____ of the world.

Read Acts 17:32-34.

How did the people of Athens respond to Paul's message?

Paul's passion for God's glory ignited in him a passion for people's salvation. Like Paul, God gives each of us as believers a passion to see others come to know Him. We must learn to speak the gospel clearly as we move to impact our culture.

Use the following truths to clearly communicate the gospel message:

Understand the Character of God...
- God is the holy, just, and gracious Creator of all things.

Understand the Sinfulness of Man...
- We are each created by God, but we are all corrupted by sin.

Understand the Sufficiency of Christ...
- Jesus alone is able to remove our sin and reconcile us to God.

Understand the Necessity of Faith...
- We are reconciled to God only through faith in Jesus.

Understand the Urgency of Eternity...
- Our eternal destiny is dependent on our response to Jesus.

As we work through this study, my prayer is that in the process of seeing issues like abortion, sex trafficking, poverty, and homosexuality in light of the gospel, you and I would be provoked with a zeal for the glory of God's name and a passion for people's salvation. My hope is that we will speak the gospel clearly as we trust the gospel completely in the culture in which God has placed us.

REFLECT

Read Isaiah 40:28.

"In the beginning, God . . ." (Gen. 1:1). Because all things begin with God and ultimately exist for God, nothing in all creation or our lives is irrelevant to Him.

Let's take a look at who God has revealed Himself to be: "I am the LORD, your Holy One," God says in Isaiah 43:15. God is the Holy One, which means that He is wholly unique and absolutely pure. Everything God is and does is right. He is without error and without equal.

This holy God is also good. "The LORD is good to all, and his mercy is over all that he has made" (Ps. 145:9). God's goodness is evident from the beginning where everything He creates is "good," culminating in man and woman, who are called "very good" (see Gen. 1). The grandeur of creation testifies to the undeniable goodness of the Creator.

God's goodness is expressed in His justice. "The LORD judges the peoples" (Ps. 7:8), and He judges them perfectly. God justifies the innocent and condemns the guilty. As a good Judge, God is outraged by injustice. God's goodness is also expressed in His grace. He shows unmerited favor to those who could never deserve it. He is compassionate and patient, desiring all people to know and enjoy His kindness, mercy, and love (see 2 Pet. 3:9).

Because God is our Creator, we belong to Him. And we are accountable to Him as our Judge. All of this puts us in a position where we are desperately in need of His grace.

Now we see the offense of the gospel coming to the forefront. Tell any modern person that there is a God who sustains, owns, defines, rules, and will one day judge him or her, and that person will balk in offense. Any man or woman would—and every man and woman has.

In what ways does your understanding of who God is impact your daily life?

How is being offended by a social issue and being offended by the gospel different?

Pray that God will give you a passion for His glory and a heart to see the gospel spread to the community in which you live.

ENGAGE

Culture Shock

When it comes to impacting the culture for Christ, it is important to know what the Bible says on major issues. The Bible is the absolute authority and our primary goal as believers is to know what God says and prioritize that over opposing viewpoints. Before the next session, read and reflect on the following verses. Make notes about what each passage says and how it connects to major issues faced in our culture.

Poverty:
- Matthew 6:3-4

- Matthew 25:34-40

Human Life:
- Matthew 6:26

- 1 Corinthians 3:16-17

Gender Roles:
- Genesis 1:27

- Ephesians 5:18-33

Racism and Diversity:
- James 2:8

- Acts 10:34-35

PREPARE

Read and respond to the following truths in preparation for your next group session.

Read 1 John 3:17.

The average American lives on more than ninety dollars per day while nearly half of the world's population lives on less than two dollars per day.[1] The standard of living which is common among us is extremely uncommon in human history. Economics professors Steve Corbett and Brian Fikkert write, "At no time in history has there ever been greater economic disparity in the world than at present." Speaking specifically about Americans, they continue, "By any measure, we are the richest people ever to walk on planet Earth."[2]

This means that average, ordinary, middle-class, working Americans live extremely wealthy lifestyles in a world surrounded by billions of extremely poor neighbors. And God has called us to love these neighbors—as ourselves. Christ's command, coupled with the depth of poverty in the world and the reality of wealth in our lives, has huge implications for the way we live. When our eyes have been opened to conditions in the world around us, our ears must be open to the question God's Word asks of us: "If anyone has the world's goods and sees his brother in need, yet closes his heart against him, how does God's love abide in him?" (1 John 3:17). This is a specific reference to followers of Christ caring for other Christians in need. However, the command of Christ in Luke 10 to love our neighbors as ourselves surely includes care not just for the believing poor but also for the unbelieving poor. If the love of God is in our hearts, then it is impossible for us to ignore the poor in our world. The gospel compels Christians in a wealthy culture to action—selfless, sacrificial, costly, countercultural action—on behalf of the poor.

What is your response to the reality of our wealth in light of the poverty in the world?

How does our understanding the issue of poverty impact our faith?

Pray that God will prepare you to see those in need and respond to them with the gospel as well as actions that show the love of God.

---

[1] United Nations Development Programme, Human Development Report 2007/2008 (New York: Palgrave Macmillan, 2007), 25.

[2] Steve Corbett & Brian Fikkert, *When Helping Hurts: How to Alleviate Poverty without Hurting the Poor...and Yourself* (Chicago, IL: Moody Publishers, 2012), 41.

SESSION 2

WEALTH

START

Trekking through a snow-covered Asian village, I saw poverty personified. As soon as we entered the village, a man stepped out of his house. He wore a tattered beige shirt and a torn brown jacket filled with holes. His name was Sameer. When I saw Sameer what stood out most was his missing eye. Not long before, his right eye had become infected. With no access to basic medicine, the infection worsened. Eventually, he lost his eye. A gaping hole now stood on the right side of Sameer's face, and the infection was spreading farther. His cheek was beginning to cave. His hearing was beginning to fail. It was evident that whatever sickness was causing the infection would soon overtake his body and eventually end his life.

As we stopped and spoke to Sameer, we were dreadfully aware of our limited ability to help him physically. As we talked, we told Sameer the story of Jesus' healing a blind man. Sameer had never heard of Jesus so we shared how Jesus healed disease as a demonstration of His power over death. We told Sameer how Jesus' death had paid the price for people's sin against God. We shared how Jesus' resurrection gives hope to all who believe in Him. Sameer smiled as he listened. Before long, we had to move on and to this day I don't know how long Sameer lived. What I do know is that God used this man with a missing eye to transform my own sight. When I looked at Sameer, I saw what happens when severe poverty turns simple illness into almost certain death.

That same day, I read Luke 10:27, which says, "You shall love the Lord your God with all your heart and with all your soul and with all your strength and with all your mind, and your neighbor as yourself." The last phrase jumped off the page, "Love your neighbor as yourself." As myself? I wondered what I would want someone to do for me if I lived in one of these villages. Wouldn't I want somebody to help me? Ignoring such urgent need is simply not an option. Yet this is exactly what so many of us in the Western church have done. We have a gaping hole in the way we see the world, and we need new sight. We need our eyes opened to the implications of the gospel for how we live.

For more insight on this week's topic, read chapters 2 & 4 of David Platt's book *Counter Culture* (Tyndale, 2015).

WATCH

Complete the viewer guide below as you watch DVD Session 2.

Over _____ _____ people live and die in desperate poverty in the world, living on less than one dollar a day.

MATERIAL RICHES IN THE CHURCH

1. The path to great _____.

2. The path to total _____.

3. The plan for _____ people.

WHAT THE GOSPEL COMPELS

1. Simplify your _____ .

2. Increase your _____ .

3. Consider your _____ .

RESPOND

Helping those in poverty is a cause that everyone can get behind. Very few people would point at the poor and claim that they don't need help. Additionally, Christians know that the call to help those in poverty is an issue the Bible speaks clearly about.

Read the following passages and list what each one teaches in regard to poverty:

- **Proverbs 21:13**

- **Proverbs 28:27**

- **James 2:14-17**

- **1 John 3:16-18**

These passages are pretty clear about how we as Christians should respond to poverty. While we may all agree that poverty is an issue we should work to end, all too often our actions don't line up with our words. We say we should help those in poverty, yet we seldom take the time or expend the effort to do so.

Let's consider the basic needs of those in poverty: Lack of food and water, lack of education, inadequate medical care, and suffering from preventable diseases. Reflect on just how many in the world struggle in desperate poverty:

There are more than 1 billion people in desperate poverty, living on less than $1 a day. Hundreds of millions of people live in slums. Hundreds of millions of people are starving. Millions of children are orphaned. Millions of widows are abandoned.

How aware were you of the amount of poverty in the world prior to this session?

What are your immediate reactions upon learning that this level of poverty exists?

The best way to understand the issue of poverty is to develop a Christ-centered view of wealth. Because we live in a culture that focuses so intently on comfort, possessions, and money, we may struggle to grasp the true nature of poverty.

How can developing a biblical view of wealth help you understand poverty better?

How do we typically view gain, achievement, and success in our culture?

Everywhere we look we're told that the path to great gain in this world is getting more—more possessions, more comfort, greater ease, better food, newer clothes, finer things. But God gives us a very different equation in Scripture.

"But godliness with contentment is great gain." –1 Timothy 6:6

Godliness with contentment is not just gain, but *great* gain. Contentment flows from a heart that trusts in the sufficiency of Christ in every area of life.

Consider how contentment impacts the following areas of your life:

	Contentment leads to...	Lack of Contentment leads to...
Money:	*Generosity*	*Greed, selfishness*
Possessions:		
Relationships:		
Future goals:		

The reality is the more we acquire, the more we want. Pursuing earthly gain will end up robbing us of our contentment in Christ and we will miss God's purpose for the resources and opportunities He has given us.

Why does the pursuit of material possessions ultimately leave you unsatisfied?

Paul explains how we can be content but he also issues a warning about the path to ruin:

But those who desire to be rich fall into temptation, into a snare, into many senseless and harmful desires that plunge people into ruin and destruction. For the love of money is a root of all kinds of evils. It is through this craving that some have wandered away from the faith and pierced themselves with many pangs. —1 Timothy 6:9-10

The path to ruin is clear: the love of money. Materialism is so ingrained in the culture we live in that it can be difficult to see how much it has been embedded into our own lives.

List the different ways materialism can take root in the life of a teenager:

Clothes: *Will only buy certain brands or shop at certain stores.*

Technology:

Family:

Relationships:

Paul tells us the path to total ruin is the desire to be rich. We must be careful here to recognize what Paul isn't saying. He isn't condemning the rich, nor is he claiming that wealth leads to materialism. He is warning us that the pursuit of wealth and money can lead us to a lack of contentment because it never satisfies our pursuit. Being rich isn't wrong, but it does heighten our need to battle materialism.

There are three ways we can pursue contentment in Christ even when we have much:

- We must flee self-confidence.
- We must flee self-centeredness.
- We must focus on God.

Which of the above is most challenging for you? Why?

God doesn't want us to avoid having good things; He wants us to prioritize Him over our possessions. God wants us to pursue Him first in all areas. Rather than spending our lives trying to become rich, important, and successful, God wants us to spend our lives enjoying His riches, glorifying His name, and sharing the gospel. We are called to use our riches, fame, and success to glorify God, but we must walk this path with caution, allowing the Holy Spirit to help us consistently choose Jesus over materialism.

The heart of the gospel is that Christ gave Himself so that we might live and experience an abundant life now, and for eternity. We are recipients of Christ's selflessness, grace, and love. So what does the gospel compel us to do in response to this reality?

1. Simplify your living.

How does a teenager simplify the way he or she lives in light of the gospel?

2. Increase your giving.

Is there anything you should sell, share, or sacrifice that might help meet the needs of others?

3. Consider your going.

Who in your sphere of influence needs to hear the gospel? Is there an opportunity for you to share the gospel with people in need (mission trip or service project)?

REFLECT

Read Matthew 6:19-21.

The grace of God in Christ compels us to invest eternally. Clearly, Jesus has put before us a choice: we can spend our wealth on short-term pleasures that we cannot keep, or we can sacrifice our wealth for long-term treasure that we'll never lose.

These thoughts remind me of my favorite part of Jesus' conversation with the rich young man. Mark 10:21 says this: "And Jesus, looking at him, loved him, and said to him, 'You lack one thing: go, sell all that you have and give to the poor, and you will have treasure in heaven; and come, follow me.'" At first this sounds like a call to sacrifice, and in one sense it is. Indeed, in this man's heart the price proved too high for him to pay—he rejected Jesus' invitation.

But upon closer examination, Jesus' words are not a call to sacrifice as much as they are a call to satisfaction. Sure, Jesus beckons the man to sell everything he has on earth, but in the next breath He promises the man everlasting treasure in eternity. It's as if Jesus is saying to him, "Give what you have to the poor; I'll give you something better." In the end, Jesus is not calling this man away from treasure; He's calling him to treasure. When we understand the passage in this way, we begin to realize that materialism is not just sinful; it's stupid. Why would we forsake eternal treasure in favor of earthly trinkets?

We must remember that this world, with both its pleasures and its poverty, is not our final home. We're living for another land, one where pleasures never fade and there is no poverty. We would be wise to open our eyes now to the spiritual and material wealth God has entrusted to us on this earth and to open our hearts to the ways He may be calling us to use that wealth for our good, the good of others, and ultimately for His glory.

How can you begin to see material possessions and wealth biblically?

How does the issue of poverty impact your community, your church, and your family?

Pray that God will give you a heart to leverage all you have for His kingdom while working wisely toward a biblical view of wealth.

ENGAGE

Step Up

When it comes to helping orphans and widows the Bible is clear:

> *"Religion that is pure and undefiled before God, the Father, is this: to visit orphans and widows in their affliction, and to keep oneself unstained from the world."* –James 1:27

Additionally, the Bible speaks to helping those in poverty:

> *"Whoever despises his neighbor is a sinner, but blessed is he who is generous to the poor."* –Proverbs 14:21

Before your next session, identify a specific way you can step in to help those in poverty, an orphan, or a widow in your community. Ask your ministry leader if your church has any widows that you might be able to connect with. Determine if there is a soup kitchen or local ministry to help those in poverty.

Use the following ideas as a starting point to step up and serve the afflicted in your community for the sake of the gospel:

- **Connect with a widow and set a regular time to help her around the house or do yard work that she might find difficult.**

- **Connect with a local home for the elderly and plan a time when you, your group, or your family might visit to simply hang out with those that live there.**

- **Determine if there is a local soup kitchen or organization that helps the poor in your community. Set a date to serve with them as they help people in need.**

- **Adopt a local family or family in your church that serves as a foster family. Volunteer to cook dinner for them or help in other ways as they take care of children in need.**

Whatever you decide to do, whether from this list or an idea of your own, remember that the service is the starting point but the gospel is the goal. Pray about how you will share the gospel with those you step up to help.

PREPARE

Read and respond to the following truths in preparation for your next group session.

Read Romans 15:1.

I am ashamed to confess that it wasn't until recently that I realized the severity of sex trafficking in the world around me. For a long time, the idea of slavery seemed to me a relic of a bygone era centuries before my time. I never could have comprehended that twenty-seven million people live in slavery today—more than at any other time in history.[3] I never could have fathomed that many of these millions are being bought, sold, and exploited for sex in what has become one of the fastest-growing industries on earth.

But even when I heard these numbers, they still seemed distant to me. As long as they were mere numbers on a page, I could distance myself from them. I could live as if they didn't exist—both the numbers and the individuals they represent. That all changed when I walked through a village in the Nupri valley of Nepal. For the first time, I came face-to-face with the horrifying reality of what happens in those mountains. When I got back to the big city of Kathmandu, I walked past restaurant after restaurant with slaves waiting outside, forced into a life of prostitution. No matter how hard I try, I can't get those sights out of my mind.

When I flew back from Nepal, I landed in Atlanta and drove on Interstate 20 to my home in Birmingham. I grew up going up and down this interstate that spans all the way to west Texas, and I had no idea that it is the "sex trafficking superhighway" of the United States. This same road that represents freedom for ten million travelers every year reflects the reality of slavery for countless girls every night. Slavery still exists. And now that we know it does, we have no excuse but to do something about it.

What is your response when you hear that there are 27 million people in slavery today?

How can you begin to pray for the people who suffer as slaves around the world?

Pray that God will prepare you to engage in this major issue facing the world.

[3]"The State Department 2013 Trafficking in Persons Report," U.S. Department of State, July 11, 2013. Accessed Nov. 26, 2014. Available from the Internet: *www.state.gov.*

SESSION 3

HUMAN LIFE

Across the world, more than forty-two million abortions occur every year. That's 150,000 every single day.[4] There is a moral disaster of mammoth proportions taking place around us. This is why I do not believe it is anywhere close to an overstatement to call abortion a modern holocaust. My intention in saying this is in no way to downplay the horror of the Holocaust in the mass murder of six million Jewish people over a few short years. But we're talking here about forty-two million children being murdered every single year. And just as German Christians didn't need to ignore the reality of what was happening in concentration camps all across their country, American Christians must not ignore the reality of what is happening in abortion clinics all across our country and around the world.

In addition to this modern holocaust, slavery, sex trafficking, and pornography demean human life every single day. In America our worship of sex has led to a widespread devaluation of women. This is apparent not only in our prostitution industry but also in our pornography industry. Additionally, the victims of sex trafficking are often used in pornography. This connection between slavery and pornography highlights the fact that by viewing pornography an individual is supporting sex trafficking and slavery.

The value of human life is being demeaned, minimized, and even negated by pornography, slavery, and abortion. As Christians we have no alternative but to do something about it. For Christians, it is the portrait of Christ in the gospel that compels us to fight for the destruction of slavery, pornography, and abortion in the world. We cannot be silent, and we must not be still. We are compelled to pray, to give, and to work to see people restored to new life. We are compelled to proclaim Christ, who alone has the ability to bring complete freedom. We are compelled to fight in all these ways with the truth of the gospel on our minds, the power of the gospel in our hearts, and the love of the gospel in our hands.

**For more insight on this week's topic, read chapters 3 & 5
of David Platt's book *Counter Culture* (Tyndale, 2015).**

[4]Susan A. Cohen, "Facts and Consequences: Legality, Incidence and Safety of Abortion Worldwide," *Guttmacher Policy Review*, Fall 2009, Vol. 12, Num. 4. Accessed Nov. 26, 2014. Available from the Internet: *www.guttmacher.org.*

WATCH

Complete the viewer guide below as you watch DVD Session 3.

THE NATURE OF GOD

1. He is the supreme _____.

2. He is the sovereign _____.

3. He is the righteous _____.

4. He is the merciful _____.

THE NATURE OF LIFE

1. We are created in the _____ of God.

2. We are created for the _____ of God.

THE NATURE OF SIN

1. The _____ of sin

2. The _____ brought about by sin

3. The _____ of sin

THE NEED FOR THE GOSPEL

1. Genesis 1-11 gives us glimpses of _____.

2. Genesis 1-11 compels us to counter _____.

RESPOND

The issues of abortion, sex slavery, and pornography all have one thing in common: they devalue and disregard human life. Our culture continues to emphasize that man defines the value of life, but the reality is that God created life and only He can define its value. In order to address difficult issues related to human life we must have a clear understanding about God. We will start by examining the nature of God.

"In the beginning, God created the heavens and the earth." –Genesis 1:1

Genesis 1:1 is filled with implications that could command all of our time and attention. The first and most important implication is that God exists. But we live in a culture that says there is no God and we were not created. Let's examine that argument for a moment because it is an unsustainable contradiction:

> » If you say something is not there, you need to have searched out all possibilities that it might be there.
> » In the case of God, to say He is not there is to say you have searched out all knowledge to see if He is there.
> » If you have searched all knowledge, then that means you have all knowledge, and by definition that makes you god, and you deny your own divinity with your statement that there is no God.

As you can see that is an unsustainable position. All of us have to at least admit the possibility that God exists.

What are some arguments against the existence of God that you have heard?

Why is the issue of God's existence difficult for some people to accept?

God exists and we can understand His nature as revealed in Genesis chapters 1 – 11.
- Genesis 1 shows us that God is the supreme Creator and the sovereign King.
- Genesis 2 and 3 show us that God is the righteous Judge.
- Genesis 3-11 show us that God is the merciful Savior.

How do these aspects of God's nature connect with the issues of abortion, pornography, and slavery?

When we understand God's nature we can begin to see how we should treat others and ourselves as His creation. Because God is Creator, King, Judge, and Savior, we can trust that He knows best. So what is our response to God? Let's take a look at the nature of life:

We are all created in the image of God.
- We are a unique reflection of God.
- We are utterly reliant upon God.
- We are ultimately responsible to God.

What does it mean to be a reflection of God?

How are we reliant on God?

Why are we responsible to God?

We are all created for the purpose of God.
- To enjoy a relationship with God.
- To rule over all creation.
- To reproduce God's glory to the ends of the earth.

How does a relationship with God fulfill His purpose for our lives?

We are created in the image of God and He defines our purpose. But in an increasingly secular, atheistic culture that says we are accountable to no one, or at most we are accountable to ourselves, the rejection of God is all too common. We reject God when we treat His creation as disposable. We reject God when we partake in pornography. We reject God when we treat others as property.

List a few ways we reject God through our actions and attitudes about life:
1. *When we put ourselves before others.*
2.
3.
4.

We have taken a look at the nature of God and the nature of life. We can see that while our response to God should be worship, it is often rejection. As we consider Genesis chapter 3, we need to keep Romans 5:12 in mind to get the full picture.

> *"Therefore, just as sin came into the world through one man, and death through sin, and so death spread to all men because all sinned." –Romans 5:12*

In Adam, we see a pattern of ourselves. We learn the nature of sin. When we understand the core of sin, we have to deal with some difficult realities. Study each of the elements at the heart of sin and answer the related questions.

Rejecting God's Word:
Whose voice will we listen to if we reject God's Word?

Spurning God's authority:
Who will rule our hearts if we spurn God's authority?

Denying God's character:
Who will we trust and obey if we deny God's character?

Sin leads us into conflict. When we chose to live outside of God's boundaries we experience:
- Conflict in our relationship with God.
- Conflict in our relationships with others.
- Conflict in our relationship with creation.

The consequences of sin are clear: there is an immediate spiritual death and an eventual physical death.

What is the connection between the core of sin, conflict of sin, and consequences of sin? List the connection below using *"rejecting God's Word"* **as an example.**

The core of sin..._rejecting God's Word._

The conflict that results is..._____.

The consequences I face are..._____.

Ultimately, sin distorts our view of God, His will for us, and His purpose for creation. This twisted view of God leads us to demean life. When we diminish and disregard human life, issues like abortion, slavery, and pornography arise.

So far in this session we have addressed difficult issues by studying the nature of God, life, and sin. We will conclude by learning the nature of salvation. No matter the situation, regardless of how dark it may be, Jesus offers grace, forgiveness, and redemption. This grace is extended not only to those suffering in these issues but also to those who are responsible. God stands available and ready to forgive. We must recognize our need for salvation.

What does God's grace mean for those trapped in slavery, who have had an abortion, or for those who have participated in pornography?

Abortion, slavery, and pornography are a result of ignoring or misunderstanding the nature of God, the nature of life, and the resulting effects of sin. Genesis 1-11 compels us to counter culture in three key ways:

1. We oppose abortion because it destroys the beauty of human life.
2. We end slavery because it denies the equality of human life.
3. We fight pornography because it denigrates the dignity of human life.

Those who claim to love and worship God cannot ignore the difficult issues we face in our culture. The proper responses we have identified clarify our way forward.

How can you begin to take action where these issues are concerned?

REFLECT

Read Mark 10:45.

My friend Jack first traveled to Nepal on a trekking expedition. He was looking forward to hiking in the Himalayas and had spent much time and money preparing for the adventure. As he began his ascension into the mountains, the first rest stop he came to brought him in contact with a variety of travelers going up and down the mountains. He noticed a couple of men who were traveling with a group of young girls. As Jack conversed with these men, they willingly told him what they were doing. They were taking these girls to the border, where they would hand them over to be sold in one of India's megacities for sexual prostitution.

Jack was stunned. As he looked at the faces of these girls, he didn't know what to do. He just started crying. In his words, "It wasn't a shallow type of cry. This was deep, real deep, like a well that frankly I haven't found the bottom of yet." In that moment, he felt more helpless than he had ever felt before. He realized that there was nothing he could do for these girls, but there was something he could do for others like them.

Jack immediately packed his bag and went down the mountain. That was over ten years ago, and in the time since that day, Jack has given his life to carrying the hope of the gospel into those Himalayan mountains. Among other things, the ministry he leads hosts a coalition of more than forty different gospel-centered organizations that are working together in Nepal to fight sex trafficking through education, prevention, rescue, and restoration. The war against sex trafficking is extremely complex and overwhelmingly difficult, but it is undoubtedly worth it for the sake of countless women and young girls in need of gospel hope.

Not everyone has the same call to ministry as Jack, but every Christian is called to stand against issues that devalue and demean human life. Being a student doesn't keep you from being able to go, give, and pray for this issue.

How can students make an impact on the issue of human life?

Which of the issues related to human life are you most passionate about? Why?

Pray that God will give you opportunities to step into the issue of human life through praying, going, and giving.

ENGAGE

Do Something

When it comes to the issue of human life, students often feel like there is little they can do. The reality is that every believer can do something. Perhaps you have never thought much about the impact you could have on the issues related to human life like abortion, slavery and pornography, but you can. Before the next session, examine the ways you might be able to impact the culture in regard to these difficult issues.

PRAY:
The greatest way you can impact the difficult issues related to human life is to pray. Pray that God will move in the lives of those considering abortion. Pray that those trapped in slavery will hear and understand the gospel and receive freedom from physical and spiritual bondage. Pray for those who perpetrate sex trafficking or participate in pornography that they will see the destructive nature of their actions and stop.

START A GROUP:
Connect with others who are interested in making an impact on the issue of human life. Discuss the ways you can work together to stop the devaluation of human life. Perhaps you could meet regularly or simply stay connected as prayer partners with the goal of seeing this issue countered for the sake of the gospel.

LOVINGLY SHARE THE MESSAGE:
Don't be silent about the value of human life. Patiently share the love and truth of God with those around you. Lead them to Scripture and encourage them to understand what God says about these issues.

Consider these suggestions and add any you may have thought of. List the actions you will take this week to counter the culture on the issue of human life.

This week I will...

1.

2.

3.

Read and respond to the following truths in preparation for your next group session.

Read 1 Corinthians 6:18.

Consider Rosaria Butterfield. For her, coming to Christ meant leaving behind her entire lifestyle. So many aspects of her life were built around her identity as a lesbian, and to alter that identity was to unravel all those details. The call to follow Christ in her life was not an invitation to receive anything she wanted in this world. It was a summons to leave behind everything she had.[5]

Consequently, we must be careful across the church not to minimize the magnitude of what it means to follow Christ. Yes, this is a gospel that beckons the homosexual woman to turn away from that lifestyle, but it is also a gospel that beckons heterosexual men to stop indulging in pornography, and singles to avoid sexual activity until marriage.

In the church today, we must make sure not to preach a gospel that merely imagines Christ as the means to a casual, conservative, comfortable Christian spin on the American dream. The gospel is a call for every one of us to die to our personal desires in order to live with unshakable trust in Christ and unswerving obedience to His Word.

God beckons us to proclaim this gospel. To care enough for one another to call each other to flee from every form of sexual immorality. Not to sit back and stay quiet because that's more convenient. Not to wait for people to come to us, but to go to them, just as Christ has come to us, in love and humility, with gentleness and patience, in the context of compassionate friendship and close relationship. To share the gospel with and to show God's love to all sorts of sexual sinners around us, knowing that eternity is at stake. For when we recognize that an everlasting heaven and an eternal hell are hanging in the balance, we realize that it is not possible to believe the gospel and to stay silent on issues of sexual sin.

What happens when we see sinfulness the way God does?

How can understanding the gospel help us confront gender issues with love and truth?

Pray that God will empower you to address those dealing with gender issues with His love and truth.

---

[5]Rosaria Champagne Butterfield, *"My Train Wreck Conversion,"* Christianity Today, February 7, 2013. Available from the Internet: www.christianitytoday.com/ct/2013/january-february/my-train-wreck-conversion.html.

SEXUALITY

Our understanding of marriage is built upon our understanding of sexuality. According to our culture, sexual differences are merely social constructions. Sure, men and women have physical distinctions, but even these can be altered, if we prefer. Aside from this, men and women are equal—and by equal, we mean identical. With this train of thought, same gender marriages make just as much sense as the traditional marriage between a man and a woman. There is no difference since we are identical, so our culture says. But what does God say?

Genesis 1:27 says, "God created man in his own image, in the image of God he created him; male and female he created them." The dignity of men and women is on display from the start. Nothing else in all creation, not even the most majestic angel, is portrayed "in the image of God." Men and women alone are like God, but not in the sense that we share all of His qualities. He is infinite; we are finite. He is divine; we are human. He is spirit; we are flesh. Yet in a way that nothing else in all creation can, we share certain moral, intellectual, and relational capacities with God. We have the power to reason, the desire to love, the ability to speak, and the capacity to make moral decisions. Most important of all, men and women have the opportunity to relate to God in a way that dogs and cats, mountains and seas, and even angels and demons can't.

Men and women share in the inexpressible worth of creatures formed in the image of God Himself. In this way, God speaks loudly from Scripture against any sort of male or female superiority or dominance in the world. For all of eternity, no gender will be greater than the other. No one should feel superior or inferior by nature of being a man or a woman. Both are beautifully—and equally—created in the image of God. But equal dignity does not eliminate distinction. As the culture wages war against the Biblical definition of marriage and attempts to redefine the roles God intended for men and women, Christians must understand God's design. No matter what schools teach, politicians proclaim, and celebrities declare, God has the final say when it comes to His creation.

**For more insight on this week's topic, read chapters 6 & 7
of David Platt's book *Counter Culture* (Tyndale, 2015).**

WATCH

Complete the viewer guide below as you watch DVD Session 4.

THREE TRUTHS ABOUT MANHOOD AND WOMANHOOD

1. God created men and women with _____ dignity.

2. God created men and women with _____ roles.

3. God created men and women as a reflection of the _____ .

THREE CONCLUSIONS ABOUT MANHOOD AND WOMANHOOD

1. All this is _____ for us.

2. All this is _____ to God.

3. All this is the essence of the _____ .

RESPOND

One of the most challenging issues facing the church today is the issue of sexuality. The culture has declared what the Bible teaches to be out of sync. Homosexuality, the roles of men and women, and the moral implications regarding each, is a cultural challenge that the church must confront. Christians must stand on the truth of God's Word while operating with the love of Christ when dealing with this issue. Let's examine Genesis 1 – 3 so that we can get a clear understanding of what God intended for men and women.

"So God created man in his own image, in the image of God he created him; male and female he created them." –Genesis 1:27

Read Genesis 1:26-36. This passage leads us to the first of three truths about manhood and womanhood:

1. God created men and women with equal dignity.

From the very beginning of the Bible, God speaks against any kind of male or female superiority or dominance. God's design is that there should be no culture where man is thought to be better than woman, or woman thought to be better than man. In any culture, any relationship, where men or women are treated as inferior, as objects to be used or abused, we are undercutting the very design of God.

Why is it important to understand that both men and women are created in the image of God?

What does our culture tell us about the roles of men and women?

What are some misconceptions our culture has about God's design for men and women?

Read Genesis 2:4-25. This passage helps us see the second truth about manhood and womanhood:

2. God created men and women with different roles.

This is where our culture tends to collide with the Biblical view of manhood and womanhood. But the reality is that the roles of both male and female are clearly defined.

- Man and woman complement one another.
- Man was created to be the head.
- Woman was created to be the helper.
- Man was created to exercise loving authority over woman.
- Woman was created to extend glad submission to man.

Why is it important to understand the roles God set in place for men and women?

How might refusing to embrace the roles God has given us impact the following:

1. Our families:

2. Our church:

3. Our society:

These first two truths are clear: God created men and women with equal dignity and different roles. The third truth we learn when studying Scripture will help us see the beauty of our equality and our differences.

3. God created men and women as a reflection of the Trinity.

God exists as one God in three persons: the Father, the Son, and the Holy Spirit. All of the persons of the Trinity are equally divine, of equal worth, and are equally worthy of praise, glory, honor, and adoration. It is here we see that God created men and women as a reflection of the Trinity.

Take a look at this connection between the Trinity and gender roles:

- The persons of the Trinity are equally divine.
- The persons of the Trinity are positionally different.
- The Father has authority over the Son.
- The Son is subject to the Father.
- This is loving authority and glad submission in the context of beautiful relationship.

What the Bible is teaching here is that there is headship and submission in God. So is that bad? Is that chauvinistic of the Father? Is that offensive to the Son? Not at all. It is good.

We are so programmed in our culture to think that authority is bad and domineering, that submission is negative and makes one inferior, but that's not true. Look at God: Authority in the Father, submission in the Son—neither of them inferior or superior, neither domineering nor denigrated, together as one, loving and leading, being loved and being led, with equal worth and value.

How does our resistance to authority impact the way we view gender roles?

How do students you interact with at school and in your community typically feel about authority? Why?

List your response to someone who says the Bible teaches women are inferior to men:

When we understand that the roles God intended for men and women are a reflection of the Trinity, we can conclude some key things concerning manhood and womanhood.

1. All of this is good for us.

- Unity in diversity: We are attracted to one another by our differences.
- Equality in the midst of intimacy: We honor one another as we enjoy one another.

How do the different roles work toward our good?

2. All of this is glorifying to God.

- We reflect His character.
- We trust His Word.

How do the different roles glorify God?

3. All of this is the essence of the gospel.

- Christ is our sacrificial groom.
- We are His submissive bride.
- God has designed the headship of men and the help of women to display the gospel of Christ to the culture around us.

How do the different roles represent the gospel?

When it comes to the issue of sexuality, gender roles, and morality we do not look to any court as the answer to the problems our culture faces. God has already defined them for us, and lawmakers or government cannot eradicate His definition. The Supreme Judge of creation has already defined the roles of men and women. These roles do not change simply to appease culture, they represent timeless truth about who God is and how God loves. The call and challenge for you and me is to live according to this truth in the time and culture in which He has placed us.

REFLECT

Read Genesis 2:4-25.

Throughout Genesis 1, there is a constant interchange between earthly creation and heavenly declaration. God creates light, and declares it good. God creates the land and the water, and declares them good. God creates the sky, planets, animals, and plants, and declares them all good. But at the end of creation, one thing is not good. Man is alone. So God makes a helper for man.

When Adam falls asleep, God takes a rib from his side and forms Eve. God doesn't need to do this—He created man from dust so He could have created woman the same way. When Adam opens his eyes, he is stunned, to say the least. The first words a human being is ever recorded saying are poetry, as Adam sings, "This at last is bone of my bones and flesh of my flesh; she shall be called Woman, because she was taken out of Man" (Gen. 2:23).

God brings man to realize that he needs someone equal to him, made with the same nature but different from him, in order to help him do things he could never do on his own. This is precisely what God gives to man in woman, and thus the stage is set for the institution of marriage. Genesis 2:24 says, "Therefore a man shall leave his father and his mother and hold fast to his wife, and they shall become one flesh." This is the beauty of God's design for man, woman, and marriage. Two dignified people, both molded in the image of their Maker. Two diverse people uniquely designed to complement one another.

Our culture declares that equality can only happen if we are identical and without distinction. But God clearly made a distinction between man and woman. As a student you face a difficult time in history as society intentionally pushes this distorted view of gender roles onto your generation and those behind you. As a Christian, you must stand on God's Word and hold true to His design for men and women.

How does the issue of gender roles impact you as a student?

How can you respond when the culture attacks your biblical view of gender roles?

Pray that God will give you opportunities to share the biblical view of gender roles and God's design for both men and women.

ENGAGE

Cultural Exam

The issue of sexuality is one of the most crucial facing our culture. The primary means through which the culture lays out its agenda is through media. This week spend time examining the various ways the culture frames gender roles. Whether through music, TV, or the way subjects are taught in school, how does the culture treat gender roles and with what purpose? List the observations you make as you examine the cultural influence.

In your school:

In music:

On television:

In the movies:

Summarize your basic observations based on what you saw and heard this week:

PREPARE

Read and respond to the following truths in preparation for your next group session.

Read Acts 17:26.

We live in a culture where we are constantly submerged in discussions about racism. We have conversations, write articles, and give speeches about how to solve racial tension in our culture. But could it be that we're grasping for solutions to a problem we've grossly misdefined?

As we've already seen, no human being is more or less human than another. All are made in God's image. It is a lack of trust in this gospel truth that has led to indescribable horrors in human history. Slavery in America, the Holocaust in Germany, the Armenian massacre in Turkey, the genocide in Rwanda, and the Japanese slaughter of six million Koreans, Chinese, Indochinese, Indonesians, and Filipinos all derived from the satanic deception of leaders and citizens who believed that they were intrinsically superior to other types of people. From the first chapter of the Bible, however, this much is clear: all men and women are made in the very likeness of God.

The Bible's storyline depicts a basic unity behind worldly diversity. From the beginning, God designed a human family that would originate from one father and one mother. From that common ancestry would come a diverse litany of clans dwelling in distant lands and developing new nations. Before long in the Bible, you see people with various skin colors with distinct cultural patterns. In this way, God's Word reminds us that regardless of the color of our skin, we all have the same roots. That's why we all need the same gospel.

Have you ever had to deal with racism? How did it impact your faith?

How does your church handle issues like diversity and racism?

Pray that God will prepare you to engage in the issue of racism with clear gospel truth and love for all people regardless of race or ethnicity.

SESSION 5

RACE

START

Addie Mae Collins, Cynthia Wesley, Carole Robertson, and Denise McNair. These four young girls suddenly lost their lives one Sunday in 1963 in a church bombing just down the street from where I serve as pastor. You may wonder why their church was bombed? And the answer has nothing to do with the kind of persecution people face around the world for their faith in Christ. No, their church was bombed because they were black.

Not long ago, I had the honor of preaching alongside the pastor at Sixteenth Street Baptist Church in the very building that had been bombed fifty years before. I stood onstage with him and other pastors in the city before a room full of black and white Christians as together we remembered that horrible event, and we renewed our commitment to one another in Christ for the sake of the gospel in our city.

When I preached my sermon that Good Friday, I had to confess the sinful tendency of my own heart to prefer one person over another based on particular commonalities. Even as I have sought to develop friendships, foster partnerships, and forge initiatives that promote unity across ethnic lines, I know there is so much more that needs to be done in my own life and in the church I lead. This is all the more evident when it comes to the related issue of immigration in our culture. There is fiery debate across the United States regarding how to address the twelve to fifteen million undocumented immigrants currently living in our country. These men, women, and children live in my community (and yours), representing various ethnicities, speaking different languages, and coming from different cultural backgrounds. We desperately need to consider how to avoid the sins of those who went before us in the Civil Rights era.

The gospel compels such social action. By the grace of God, we must work to overcome prejudicial pride in our lives, families, and churches. Moreover, with the wisdom of God, we must labor to respect immigration laws in our country as responsible citizens while loving immigrant souls in our community.

For more insight on this week's topic, read chapter 8 of David Platt's book *Counter Culture* (Tyndale, 2015).

WATCH

Complete the viewer guide below as you watch DVD Session 5.

From the very beginning, the story line of the Bible depicts a basic _____ behind worldly diversity.

Fundamentally, we're all part of the same _____ .

A PICTURE OF UNITY AND DIVERSITY

1. See the _____ God has made.

2. See the _____ Christ has paid.

3. See the _____ God has prepared.

RESPOND

We live in a culture where we're constantly submerged in discussions about racism. We have conversations and host forums, sponsor debates and foster dialogues, write articles and give speeches about how to solve racial tension in our culture. But could it be that we're grasping for solutions to a problem that we've totally misdefined? And could it be that the gospel not only counters culture on this issue, but also reshapes the conversation about race altogether?

"After this I looked, and behold, a great multitude that no one could number, from every nation, from all tribes and peoples and languages, standing before the throne and before the Lamb, clothed in white robes, with palm branches in their hands, and crying out with a loud voice, 'Salvation belongs to our God who sits on the throne, and to the Lamb!'"
–Revelation 7:9-10

Read Revelation 7:9-17. This passage is a picture of where all of eternity is headed. Notice the beauty of unity and diversity coupled together. This is a stark contrast from our world today. Think about your current community.

Do you see evidence of racism in your school and community? If so, give examples.

How does your community or school try to counter the issue of racism if it exists? If it doesn't exist, why do you think that is?

Determine the degree of racism present in each sphere of your community.
(1 = racism is not present at all and 4 = racism is very present)

My family (including extended family):	1	2	3	4
My neighborhood:	1	2	3	4
My school:	1	2	3	4
My city:	1	2	3	4
My state:	1	2	3	4

Regardless of the level of racism you experience, Revelation 7 describes a future in which we will experience the unity and diversity God created without any bias or racist thought. Let's focus on a few key things that this passage reveals.

1. See the promise God has made.

"These are the clans of the sons of Noah, according to their genealogies, in their nations, and from these the nations spread abroad on the earth after the flood." –Genesis 10:32

"Now the LORD said to Abram, 'Go from your country and your kindred and your father's house to the land that I will show you. And I will make of you a great nation, and I will bless you and make your name great, so that you will be a blessing. I will bless those who bless you, and him who dishonors you I will curse, and in you all the families of the earth shall be blessed.'" –Genesis 12:1-3

How does the picture in Revelation 7:9-17 fulfill God's promise in Genesis?

God's promise and purpose was to show His glory among all people. All of history is headed toward the day when worshipers from every race, tribe, and tongue will assemble as one to give God the praise He is due. As a result we are to:

- Work for ethnic harmony because of God's purpose in all of history.
- Understand that God is most glorified when His people are most unified.

It is critical that we understand something about the gospel and diversity: God doesn't bring us all together around a certain position; He brings us together around His Son. When we prioritize Jesus, unity is the only true response.

2. See the price Christ has paid.

Remember the passage from Revelation 7? This multitude around the throne is wearing white robes and they're crying out, "Salvation belongs to our God and to the Lamb." The Lamb being referred to is Jesus Christ. And one of the elders asks, "Who are these, clothed in white robes, and from where have they come?" and the response is, "These are the ones who have washed their robes and made them white in the blood of the Lamb."

Now that's a strange image. How do you wash your clothes in red blood and have them come out spotless white? The answer takes us back to the core of who God is and what God has done. Jesus shed His blood for people of every tribe and tongue.

What does the shedding of blood for all people say about God's view of diversity and race?

Jesus offers salvation to all, but currently there are over 6,000 people groups still unreached with the gospel and over 2,000 languages that still have no Bible.

What do these statistics tell us about our call to reach the world with the gospel?

List ways you can impact these statistics in your own family, school, and community.

Family:

School:

Community:

Knowing that Christ died for all, yet seeing that so many are still unreached, we cannot sit back. As a people who have been reached with the gospel, we must give our lives reaching peoples who have never heard the message of Jesus Christ.

We have seen the promise God has made and the price Christ has paid. In order to truly understand the biblical view on diversity, unity, and racism we must also look to the future.

3. See the place God has prepared.

What do you think about when you think of spending eternity in heaven?

Revelation 7:15-17 shows us the place that God has prepared for us in which we will no longer experience racism but true unity and diversity.

> *"Therefore they are before the throne of God, and serve him day and night in his temple; and he who sits on the throne will shelter them with his presence. They shall hunger no more, neither thirst anymore; the sun shall not strike them, nor any scorching heat. For the Lamb in the midst of the throne will be their shepherd, and he will guide them to springs of living water, and God will wipe away every tear from their eyes."*
> *–Revelation 7:15-17*

The future God has for those who follow Him is amazing. Not just because we will no longer hunger or thirst, but because we will share in the presence of Jesus Christ, the Lamb. We will worship together in perfect harmony. There will be eternal enjoyment of the presence of God where we will stand, sing, serve, and be fully satisfied in Him forever.

What are three things you need to be doing now knowing that everyone will either spend eternity in heaven worshiping Jesus or in hell separated from God forever?

In the end, we are all immigrants ourselves, aren't we? I'm not merely referring to our ancestors who may have migrated to America many years ago. I'm referencing the very essence of what it means to be a Christian. The Bible calls believers in Christ "sojourners and exiles" who "desire a better country" and are "seeking a homeland," a "city that is to come." Christians are migrants on this earth, and the more we get involved in the lives of immigrants, the better we will understand the gospel.

By the sheer grace of God in the gospel, we are compelled to resist ethnic pride and prejudice and to reflect truth and grace as we look forward to the day when "a great multitude that no one could number, from every nation, from all tribes and peoples and languages" (Rev. 7:9) will stand as one redeemed race to give glory to the all-sovereign King who ransomed us by His blood.

For now, we work together for unity in our diversity.

Read 1 Peter 2:11; Hebrews 11:13-16; 13:14.

I have a friend named Tyler who pastors in Arizona. Amid the massive influx of immigrants into his community and surrounded by political discussions in his state, Tyler and the church he leads have decided to engage this issue with gospel perspective and compassion. Together they began providing food and clothing to migrant workers through a variety of different ministries. These ministries paved the way for personal relationships to develop with immigrants, opening other doors for members of the church not just to love but to learn from these workers and their families. This has obviously involved more time and resources, but in Tyler's words, "It wasn't long before our people began donating more than food—they started to donate their lives." This eventually led to the construction of a community center in the heart of a Latino neighborhood that is now filled weekly with English classes, after-school programs, life-skills training, and Bible studies.

In all of this, Tyler and his congregation have engaged in hundreds of conversations about Jesus and have seen God change lives. But it hasn't been easy. Tyler commented, "Our work has been affirmed by many but has also been met with criticism from both inside and outside the church." One of the things I appreciate about Tyler is his willingness to both listen to and learn from such criticism. In his words, "We've found that it's important to pause and listen to the critiques of respectable people with legitimate concerns. We especially need to listen to those who challenge us on the grounds that our work counteracts the common good. If their concern is valid, we should respond and adjust accordingly. If, however, they are misguided, we should clarify our intentions and continue the work to which we have been called."[6]

No one can expect to engage in ministry like this and not experience challenges like these. What I admire most about Tyler and his church is the way they are not afraid to step off the sidelines at great cost to apply the gospel to this pressing social need in our day.

What is God teaching you about the issue of racism, diversity, and unity?

Pray that God will give you and your church a heart for biblical unity so that the gospel may be lived out and shared with everyone regardless of their ethnicity or socio-economic background.

[6]Tyler Johnson & Jim Mullins,*"One Church's Journey on Immigration,"* The Gospel Coalition (blog), October 31, 2012. Available from the Internet: *http://thegospelcoalition.org/blogs/tgc/2012/10/31/one-churchs-journey-on-immigration/.*

ENGAGE

Letter From Birmingham Jail

Martin Luther King, Jr. was a key leader in speaking out against racism and civil rights abuses. Arrested and in prison in the city of Birmingham, Alabama, King penned a letter that spoke to the issue of racism and specifically the way the church and pastors treated the cause. Spend some time this week either reading or listening to the letter and list key points to take away from Dr. King's words. You can access video (with audio) and/or the text of the letter by searching the Internet for "Letter from Birmingham Jail."

What is Dr. King saying in his letter?

How would you respond to Dr. King's letter?

How does the gospel speak to the issue of racism?

Are there changes you need to make in the way you view diversity based on what you've learned?

> ## "INJUSTICE ANYWHERE IS A THREAT TO JUSTICE EVERYWHERE."[7]
> ### DR. MARTIN LUTHER KING, JR.

---

[7] Martin Luther King, Jr. *"Letter From Birmingham Jail,"* 1963 (online, cited December 1, 2014). Available from the Internet: *http://web.cn.edu/kwheeler/documents/Letter_Birmingham_Jail.pdf*

PREPARE

Read and respond to the following truths in preparation for your next group session.

Read 2 Corinthians 5:18-20.

It is an essential part of the human experience to ask and answer questions like "Where did I come from?" and "Why am I here?" and then to act in accordance with the conclusions.

Obviously, different people will make different determinations regarding what to believe, who to worship, and how to live. This is a choice that God has devised all people to possess, for from the beginning God has given men and women the freedom to decide whether to worship Him. Adam and Eve were not forced into faith or coerced into obedience when they dwelled with God in the Garden. Instead, part of their humanness was the ability (and opportunity) to act of their own will, a God-given privilege that eventually resulted in their decision to disobey Him. But it was their decision, for even in His divine sovereignty, God did not (and does not) remove human responsibility.

This reality becomes all the more clear in the rest of Scripture, specifically in the life and ministry of Jesus. Never do we see Jesus forcing faith onto people. Instead, He teaches doctrine, tells stories, and then invites men and women to receive or reject Him. In response, people listen to Him, reason with Him, argue with Him, and often abandon Him. In the end, the gospel message is fundamentally a matter of invitation, not coercion.

For this reason, those who understand and believe the gospel advocate the free exercise of faith. But how does the expression of faith look? If we believe that Jesus died to provide a way of salvation then we must act upon this belief. There are millions worldwide who need to hear the message of the gospel. The call for every believer is to take the gospel to the entire world.

How have you responded to Christ's call to take the gospel to the world?

What are some basic steps you can take to start or to continue sharing the gospel in your community and beyond?

Pray that God will give you opportunities to share the gospel regardless of persecution you may face.

SESSION 6

FAITH

START

Eerie. That's the only word that comes to mind when I think about standing a hundred yards from North Korean soldiers who were staring right back at me with weapons in their hands. I was in the demilitarized zone (DMZ), a small strip of land that cuts the Korean peninsula in half, separating the North and the South. Approximately 150 miles long and 2.5 miles wide, it serves as a buffer between these two countries and the allies they represent.

I stood in the Joint Security Area, the only part of the DMZ that allows North and South Korean forces to stand face-to-face with one another. Years ago, this village was designated as the location where negotiations between the two countries would take place. In the center is a small blue building where international meetings occur. Inside, there is a conference table with a white line running down the middle of it. During official discussions, South Korean officials sit on one side of that line while North Korean officials sit opposite them.

North Korea has a heinous human rights record. Food deprivation, forced labor, systematic torture, and public executions all characterize this communist country. For years, North Korea has been at the top of the World Watch List, a ranking of fifty countries that exposes the places where Christians are most persecuted in the world.

Freedom of religion for North Koreans is nonexistent. And though the conditions may not be as severe, the same can be said for multitudes of men and women in many other nations. The denial of this freedom affects people of different faiths, yet followers of Christ comprise the most widely persecuted religious group in the world. So how does the gospel compel us to live in a world of religious persecution? And does the gospel compel us to act on behalf of those who suffer for other faiths—Jews, Muslims, Hindus, Buddhists, animists, or atheists? The more we consider these questions, the more we realize that religious liberty is a rare commodity in the world, and one which is increasingly uncommon in our own culture.

For more insight on this week's topic, read chapters 9 & 10 of David Platt's book *Counter Culture* (Tyndale, 2015).

WATCH

Complete the viewer guide below as you watch DVD Session 6.

THE POWER OF THE GOSPEL

1. As we believe the gospel with deep-seated _____ in our lives, let's proclaim the gospel with death-defying _____ in the world.

- Those who _____ the gospel _____ the gospel.

2. As we live to _____ God's grace among more people, let's long to _____ God's glory among all people.

- What drives passion for getting the gospel to unreached people is not guilt; it's _____.

3. As we continually envision eternal _____ with God, let's joyfully embrace earthly _____ from God.

- God's purpose is _____.

- Our hope is _____.

RESPOND

As we begin this session let's reflect on what we concluded with in the last session. There are 11,000 different people groups in the world with more than 6,000 still classified as unreached with the gospel.[8] This is a staggering reality.

> *"Since we have the same spirit of faith according to what has been written, 'I believed, and so I spoke,' we also believe, and so we also speak, knowing that he who raised the Lord Jesus will raise us also with Jesus and bring us with you into his presence. For it is all for your sake, so that as grace extends to more and more people it may increase thanksgiving, to the glory of God." —2 Corinthians 4:13-16*

Read 2 Corinthians 4:13-18. In the midst of the great need for the spread of the gospel in our world today, Paul's words in this passage should stir our hearts.

What do these verses say about our call to reach the world with the gospel?

How can students be intentional about reaching the world with the gospel? Be specific.

When it comes to taking the gospel to the world, no Christian is exempt. Consider the case of C.T. Studd. He was a wealthy Englishman who upon coming to Christ sold everything he had to take the gospel to the nations. Many sought to dissuade him, but he went anyway, first to China and then to India. At the age of 50, he decided retirement was not an option for the Christian, so he spent his remaining years proclaiming the gospel in Sudan. He died there and his grave became a steppingstone for what was known as the Worldwide Evangelization Crusade, spreading the gospel across Africa, Asia, and South America.

How can students have a heart like C.T. Studd toward reaching their world?

[8] *See www.peoplegroups.org and www.joshuaproject.net for information and statistics on people groups.*

List some challenges students face when stepping out to make an impact for the gospel in the following places:

School:

Community:

World:

We find three key factors in 2 Corinthians 4:13-18 about having faith that counters the culture we live in.

1. As we believe the gospel with deep-seated conviction in our lives, let's proclaim the gospel with death-defying confidence in the world.

What did Paul mean when he said that believing automatically leads to speaking?

The reality is that when you believe this gospel, you speak this gospel. When you believe the resurrection of Christ, you proclaim the resurrection of Christ. Privatized faith in a resurrected King is practically inconceivable. We believe and so we speak. We are motivated to do so even when we suffer.

In 2 Corinthians 4:13, Paul refers to a psalm to describe his motivation for perseverance in gospel mission. Psalm 116:10 is a song of deliverance, written by a psalmist who had been saved from what looked like certain death, and he wrote: "I believed, even when I spoke: 'I am greatly afflicted.'" The point is this: suffering cannot silence the spirit of faith.

Discuss the meaning of the statement: "suffering cannot silence the spirit of faith."

What are examples you have you seen of people who maintained faith in the midst of suffering?

In 2 Corinthians 4, we continue to see the way God empowers us to have faith that counters the culture. **Read 2 Corinthians 4:15 again.**

2. As we live to extend God's grace among more people, let's long to exalt God's glory among all peoples.

The goal is two-fold: to share the grace of God with the world and to exalt God in the process.

How does sharing the gospel give glory to God?

What are reasons that followers of Christ might not share the gospel?

When it comes to sharing the gospel we can be driven by the wrong motivations and so this two-fold goal helps us see the truth that we do it for God's glory and nothing else. All too often we are driven to share out of guilt:

- We feel guilty that we have the gospel and they don't.
- We feel guilty because we have all these resources and they don't.
- Some may ask, "Aren't you just guilting people into going overseas to unreached peoples?"

Have you ever felt like you were guilted into sharing the gospel?

How can we learn to share the gospel for the sake of God's glory rather than out of guilt?

We have seen in the study of 2 Corinthians 4:13-18 how Paul calls us to have a faith that counters the culture with confidence and passion for God's glory. Finally we see a third exhortation in the final verses of the passage. **Read 2 Corinthians 4:16-18 again.**

3. As we continually envision eternal glory with God, let's joyfully embrace earthly suffering from God.

The truth is that we will experience affliction and persecution when we counter the culture around us. This is a call to confront those in our culture with both God's love and God's truth. Nothing is more apparent in this challenge than the fact that there will be resistance.

What kinds of persecution do students face in our culture when sharing the love and truth of God with others?

What resistance to the truth of God have you experienced in your school and/or community?

The battle between the god of this world and the God over this world rages every second of every day. Christ-followers are right in the middle of the battle preaching Christ.

Do you feel like your faith puts you in a difficult position in your school/community? Explain.

The more passionate we are about spreading the gospel to every people group in the world, the more we will suffer; not because we're seeking suffering, but because we're speaking Christ, and suffering for the gospel accompanies the spread of the gospel.

In a country where even our own religious liberty is increasingly limited, our suffering brothers and sisters beckon us not to let the cost of following Christ in our culture silence our faith. Privatized Christianity is no Christianity at all, for it is practically impossible to know Christ and not proclaim Christ—to believe His Word when we read it in our homes or churches, and not obey it in our communities. We must always remember that while our citizenship officially belongs to the government, our souls ultimately belong to God.

REFLECT

Read Matthew 28:19-20.

I stood at the Bagmati River in South Asia where every day funerals are held and bodies are burned. It is the custom among these Hindu people when family or friends die to take their bodies within twenty-four hours to the river, where they lay them on funeral pyres and set the pyres ablaze. In so doing, they believe their friend or family member will be helped in their cycle of reincarnation. As I saw this scene before me, I stood in downcast silence. For as I watched these flames overtake the bodies, I knew based on Scripture that I was witnessing at that moment a physical reflection of an eternal reality. Tears streamed down my face as I realized that most if not all of the people I was watching burn had died without ever hearing the good news of how they can live forever.

When will the concept of unreached peoples become intolerable to the church? What will it take to wake us up? This cannot be conceivable for people who confess the gospel. For if this gospel is true, and if our God is worthy of the praise of all people, then we must spend our lives and mobilize our churches for the spread of Christ's love to unreached people groups all around the world. Jesus has not given us a commission to consider; he has given us a command to obey.

That command involves sacrifice on our part. If we have this much access to the gospel in our culture, and there is this much absence of the gospel in other cultures, then surely God is leading many more of us to go to those places. If God calls us to stay in this culture, then surely He is leading us to live simply and give sacrificially so that as many people as possible can go. We know that the task before us will be trying. These people groups are unreached for a reason: they are difficult and dangerous to reach. But the gospel compels us in grace to risk our lives, our futures, our plans, and our possessions to proclaim the greatest news in order to meet people's greatest need.

Why are we so indecisive when it comes to reaching people with the gospel?

How can we help one another have a passion to glorify God in our culture and beyond?

Pray that God will empower you to live a life of faith that counters the culture with the love of God and the truth of God.

ENGAGE

What's Your Story?

The challenge of reaching the world with the gospel is great. But our God is greater and He has equipped us to take the message to those who have not yet heard. The International Mission Board is an entity that works toward the spread of the gospel to the 6,000 people groups or 1.7 billion people who have yet to hear it. This week watch a few commission stories to learn more about what it is to have a burden to reach the unreached for the sake of the gospel. You can find stories at: http://www.commissionstories.com/stories

After watching the stories list your response to the following:

How will I take the gospel to my family this week?

Potential persecution I might face:

How will I take the gospel to my friends and community this week?

Potential persecution I might face:

How will I further the gospel in my country this week?

Potential persecution I might face:

How will I further the gospel around the world this week?

Potential persecution I might face:

PREPARE

Read and respond to the following truths in preparation for developing a plan of action.

Read Luke 9:57-62

I have sought to share deep personal and pastoral burdens that weigh heavy on my heart. I know many followers of Christ who possess similar passions regarding the same realities. The oppression of the poor, the abortion of children, the neglect of orphans and widows, the trafficking of slaves, the significance of marriage and sexuality, the need for ethnic equality, and the importance of religious liberty are all mammoth issues in our lives, families, churches, and culture. My hope is that if you didn't feel a burden for these things before you started this study, you do now.

Yet I don't want these burdens on my heart to terminate with the words of this Bible study. I don't want to waste the life God has granted me or the opportunities God has given me to apply the gospel by which God has saved me in the culture where God has placed me.

I'm guessing you don't want to waste your life in this culture either. So I'm compelled to ask you a question based Luke 9:57-62. The three men in this passage were potential followers of Jesus, but from all we can tell in this text, it seems as though Jesus talked them out of following Him. The reason this passage comes to mind at the close of this study is because this is essentially the decision you and I are considering at this moment in our culture. Are we going to follow Jesus? Not, are we going to bow our heads, say a prayer, read the Bible, go to church, and give a tithe while we get on with the rest of our lives? But, are we going to follow Jesus with all our lives, no matter where He leads us to go, how much He calls us to give, or what the cost may be for us?

How has this study impacted your life and view of the culture?

How can you live out a commitment to counter the culture with the gospel?

Pray that God will empower you to live a life that counters the culture for the sake of the gospel.

PLAN OF ACTION

COUNTERING CULTURE

Counter Culture is a call to social action. However, we don't have to look very far in church history to be reminded that an increased emphasis on social issues has often been accompanied by a decreased emphasis on gospel truths. The so-called "social gospel" of the twentieth century was in essence a substitute gospel that stripped Christianity of the core tenets of orthodoxy and set many churches on a trajectory toward theological liberalism and biblical heresy. For this reason, I believe it necessary to state from the start that when I talk about social action, my aim is in no way to minimize the gospel. Instead, I want to magnify the gospel as the very reason why we confront social issues in our culture.

Consider the gospel: the good news that the God of the universe has looked upon relentlessly rebellious and hopelessly sinful men and women and has sent Jesus, God in the flesh, to bear His wrath against sin on the cross and to show His power over sin in the Resurrection so that all who turn from themselves and trust in Him can be reconciled to God for all of eternity.

To that end you need to focus on the gospel as you develop a plan to counter culture in your school and community. Will you take this opportunity to create some intentional steps toward impacting the culture?

DEVELOP YOUR PLAN

Your plan to counter culture will need to have practical ways in which you can engage each issue for the sake of the gospel. Examine the six areas of cultural challenge that have been covered in this study and respond with actions you will take:

1. HOW WILL I INTENTIONALLY ENGAGE CULTURE?

Recognize the issues your culture is dealing with on a personal level. Become familiar with issues in your school and community.

What are the top two or three issues that most impact my community?

You may live in an area that poverty is not as prevalent or you may see the difficulties brought on by racism every day. Regardless of your context, you need to know what the major areas of impact are so you can step into them with the gospel.

In what areas am I most able to make a difference?

Once you know the issues that are at the forefront in your community and school you will need to assess which ones you are best equipped to deal with. While every Christian is called to stand for truth in each of these cultural challenges, you may be more capable of making a difference in some rather than others. Identify your strengths and take steps to make an impact there first.

What is the first basic step I can take toward countering culture in my community?

It can be overwhelming to stand up to the culture on major issues like the ones listed in this study. Focus first on what you can do now, today, that will have an impact. Take the small steps necessary to accomplish the goal over time.

2. HOW WILL I ENGAGE THE ISSUE OF POVERTY, WIDOWS, AND ORPHANS?

Get to know the areas of impact you can have on the impoverished, the orphans, and the widows in your community. You may have opportunities at your church or through city or regional organizations.

How can I best engage the poor in my community?
Is there a soup kitchen or shelter that you could serve? Are there initiatives that your church has implemented to reach the poor in your city? Keep in mind that serving the poor must not stop at simply giving food and shelter, but must involve the gospel. More than serving a person's physical needs, you are called to serve their spiritual needs.

Is there a widow or home for the elderly that I can serve?
Imagine the difference you could make by serving a widow who may not be able to take care of her house or yard. Suggest that your family or church group adopt a widow and commit to serving her. Again, the goal is to do more than just service projects and helping with chores. These are good things but without the gospel they do not fully serve the widow you are helping.

How can I help orphans?
While you aren't able to adopt as a teenager, you can create awareness, build friendships, and encourage others who are able to adopt. You can also pray for and give support toward efforts that impact adoption.

3. HOW WILL I ENGAGE THE ISSUE OF HUMAN LIFE?
Issues like abortion, slavery, and pornography are difficult, especially for students. But you can and should plan to counter the culture on these issues.

How will I stand against slavery, abortion and pornography?
While these are difficult issues, they are issues that affect teenagers. Understanding the reasons each of these issues devalue human life will empower you to share that truth with others. Additionally, making the connection between slavery and pornography will equip you to help others understand why it devalues human life.

How can I be personally accountable?

With an issue like pornography, it is important to have accountability in your own life. Team up with a Christian friend, parent, or ministry leader to remain accountable to purity. Look into software programs that can help keep you accountable as you use the Internet.

How can I counter the issue of abortion?

Whether you determine to pray for those dealing with the decision to choose life or abortion, or you connect with organizations that help these women, you can step into the issue.

4. HOW WILL I ENGAGE THE ISSUE OF GENDER ROLES AND MORALITY?

Understanding that God created men and women differently for a reason doesn't diminish the equality of their roles. While they are certainly equal, they are not identical.

How can I address the issue of gender roles with other students?

One of the major issues facing our culture today is the issue of gender roles. As you are confronted on this issue, how can you present the love of God and the truth of God?

Who do I know that needs to hear the gospel?

No matter what the issue is the gospel offers grace and forgiveness. Who do you know that needs to hear the gospel? Think of someone that you might be able to share with and begin to pray for God to work in that person's heart and open doors for you to share.

How can I encourage my group or church to extend love to those who are walking in disobedience to God?

Those who are caught in a lifestyle that is contrary to Scripture such as homosexuality need to know about the love and grace of God. Likewise, they need to hear the truth of God as it applies to their lives. Discuss with your pastor or ministry leader the ways in which you might be able to offer love and truth to those who need it.

5. HOW WILL I ENGAGE THE ISSUE OF RACISM, DIVERSITY, AND UNITY?

As we have seen in the book of Revelation, the future awaiting all followers of Jesus is one of unity and diversity. Working toward unity here and now is the biblical response to racism. The gospel is good news for all people regardless of race, and Christians should lead the way toward building unity.

Identify areas in which I, my family, and my community might need to grow in terms of diversity.

Before you step in to address the culture on this issue, assess your own potential bias. Evaluate your family and church when it comes to the issue of racism. With a fresh eye you may be able to see that there are subtle ways in which unity is difficult to achieve. Pray and seek to eliminate the racism that might be present, and pray for others to have their eyes opened to the God who loves all people regardless of race or ethnicity.

In what areas might my family, church, or community become more diverse?

Do the people in your student ministry reflect the community or just a segment of the community? Work with your student pastor or group leader to identify ways you might become more inclusive of those who aren't involved.

What is the first basic step I can take toward building diversity and unity in my family, community, and church?

It may be a difficult conversation you have with a parent or sibling. It might be intentional prayer for hearts to be open. Regardless, what is the first practical step you can take toward biblical unity and diversity?

6. HOW WILL I ENGAGE THE ISSUE OF FAITH AND MISSIONS?

Your faith in Christ leads you to be missional, to live out the gospel every day. Rather than mere words, followers of Jesus are called to action. Making a difference in your community, your country, and around the world for the sake of the gospel is not a suggestion; it is a command. It's time to step up and boldly engage in Kingdom work.

What can I do locally to impact my community for Jesus?

Regardless of whether or not you ever plan to go to another country to impact the world with the gospel, there are opportunities right in your community to make an impact. Work with your church to determine the best ways to impact your community with the gospel.

How can I leverage my resources, time, and talents toward being missional?

Just because you are a student doesn't mean you can't make a difference. Whether you support a mission organization that helps those around the world in need, or commit to pray for an unreached people group, God has called all believers to live out their faith in reaching the world.

WRITE YOUR PLAN

Over the course of this study you have learned about the major issues in our culture. In each session you have been asked in the "ENGAGE" section to complete an activity related to the issue covered. Go back through the study and identify your responses in each activity and use them as a guide to finalize your personal plan to counter culture.

1. HOW WILL I INTENTIONALLY ENGAGE CULTURE?

2. HOW WILL I ENGAGE THE ISSUE OF POVERTY, WIDOWS, AND ORPHANS?

3. HOW WILL I ENGAGE THE ISSUE OF HUMAN LIFE?

4. HOW WILL I ENGAGE THE ISSUE OF GENDER ROLES AND MORALITY?

5. HOW WILL I ENGAGE THE ISSUE OF RACISM, DIVERSITY, AND UNITY?

6. HOW WILL I ENGAGE THE ISSUE OF FAITH AND MISSIONS?

Reflect on your plan to counter culture. Pray through what God has called you to do and continue to stand for God's truth while presenting God's love to those around you.